MY FIRST BRITANNICA

Folklore
and Religions

5

ENCYCLOPÆDIA
Britannica®

CHICAGO   LONDON   NEW DELHI   PARIS   SEOUL   SYDNEY   TAIPEI   TOKYO

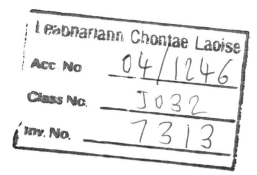
International Standard Book Number: 1-59339-048-3 (set)
International Standard Book Number: 1-59339-053-X (volume 5)

My First Britannica:
Volume 5: Folklore and Religions 2004

Britannica.com may be accessed on the Internet at http://www.britannica.com.

Folklore and Religions

TABLE OF CONTENTS

Golden Buddha at Thiksey Monastery, Ladakh, India
© Stephanie Colasanti/Corbis

I N T R O D U C T I O N

What was Excalibur?
Who stabbed a one-eyed man-eating giant? Where was Buddha born?
What happened when Moses approached the Red Sea?

In Volume 5, *Folklore and Religions,* you'll discover answers to these questions and many more. Through pictures, articles, and fun facts, you'll learn about the many legends, myths, fables, and beliefs long cherished throughout the world.

To help you on your journey, we've provided the following signposts in *Folklore and Religions*:

■ **Subject Tabs**—The coloured box in the upper corner of each right-hand page will quickly tell you the article subject.

■ **Search Lights**—Try these mini-quizzes before and after you read the article and see how much - *and how quickly* - you can learn. You can even make this a game with a reading partner. (Answers are upside down at the bottom of one of the pages.)

■ **Did You Know?**—Check out these fun facts about the article subject. With these surprising 'factoids', you can entertain your friends, impress your teachers, and amaze your parents.

■ **Picture Captions**—Read the captions that go with the photos. They provide useful information about the article subject.

■ **Vocabulary**—New or difficult words are in **bold type**. You'll find them explained in the Glossary at the back of this volume. And there's a complete listing of all Glossary terms in the set in the **Reference Guide and Index**, Volume 13.

■ **Learn More!**—Follow these pointers to related articles throughout the set.

And don't forget: If you're not sure where to start, where you saw something before, or where to go next, the **Reference Guide and Index** (Volume 13) will point the way.

Have a great trip!

MY FIRST BRITANNICA

Stories of Wonders
and Everyday Life

SEARCH LIGHT

Which of the following is a story about ordinary people doing unusual things?
a) myth
b) fable
c) folktale

6

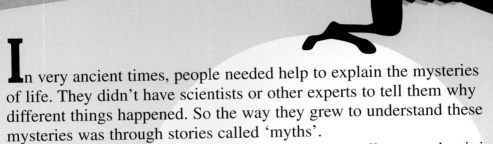

In very ancient times, people needed help to explain the mysteries of life. They didn't have scientists or other experts to tell them why different things happened. So the way they grew to understand these mysteries was through stories called 'myths'.

Today when we call something a myth, we usually mean that it isn't true. But that's often because we don't believe the very old stories. People used to believe in myths very strongly.

Some of the most familiar European myths come from ancient Greece. The gods and goddesses of Greek religion all had stories about them that explained just why things were the way they were.

World religions today have their own mythologies. Hinduism, for example, is filled with wondrous tales of gods and heroes, such as the elephant-headed god Ganesha, who represents good luck. One Bible story tells how Moses led the original Jews out of slavery in Egypt. And the famous stories of Jesus stand as examples to Christians of a perfect life.

Myths are closely related to several other kinds of stories that teach us lessons. These include folktales, legends, fables, and fairy tales.

Folktales are very much like myths, though they are usually about ordinary characters in unusual situations.

Legends resemble folktales and myths, but they're usually linked to a particular place or person that is real or imaginary.

Fables teach lessons by telling stories with animal characters.

Fairy tales sometimes carry a message about right and wrong. But often they're simply exciting, magical stories.

LEARN MORE! READ THESE ARTICLES…
FOLK MUSIC (VOLUME 3)
A GREEK LEGEND: ODYSSEUS AND THE CYCLOPS (VOLUME 5)
RELIGION (VOLUME 5)

Answer: c) folktale

DID YOU KNOW?
There are some real dragons alive today. They are the giant Komodo dragons, 3-metre-long lizards that live in Indonesia.

SEARCH LIGHT

Which of the following is not breathed out by dragons?
a) ice
b) fire
c) mist

Beasts of
Fire and Mist

According to a popular story, there was once a terrible dragon in a city where many people lived. It had huge wings like a bat. The flapping of its wings could be heard for miles. It could kill an ox with a single blow. Its eyes flashed and it breathed fire.

Every year, the people of the city had to offer the dragon a girl to eat, or it would kill everyone. One year it was the turn of Princess Sabra to face the dragon. George, the youngest and bravest of the champions who protected the Christian church, came forward to save her. He wounded the dragon with his magic sword, Ascalon. The princess threw her sash around the dragon's neck and pulled the beast to the marketplace, where George killed it with a single blow. George later became the **patron saint** of England.

People used to believe in all kinds of dragons. The beasts roamed the land, swishing their great scaly tails. They flashed fiery glances from their enormous eyes. They blew rings of poisonous smoke and breathed out flames of fire without ever burning their tongues!

In China and other Asian countries, on the other hand, the dragon, or *long*, is considered good, lucky, and a powerful protector of people. The Chinese emperors adopted the dragon as their symbol. Dragons are linked with water and they breathe out mist and clouds instead of smoke and fire. You can see huge, colourful paper dragons being carried during Chinese New Year and other celebrations. Maybe stories of dragons started because people found dinosaur bones and didn't know what they were. The bones would have looked like they came from monsters.

LEARN MORE! READ THESE ARTICLES...

Answer: a) ice

The Monkey Court

Once two young friends were walking along together when they saw a large piece of meat. Each boy thought he had seen the meat first, so each thought he deserved to have it. The two argued over the meat. And though they both thought it right to share, they thought that the other should take the smaller portion. They agreed to take their **dispute** to the Monkey Court.

Now Monkey saw them coming and he realized that here was a real chance for him. So he put on his wisest face and listened patiently to their story.

When the two boys had finished talking, Monkey said, 'I shall divide the meat equally between you.' With that, Monkey tore the meat in two and was about to hand it over when he noticed that the two pieces were uneven.

SEARCH LIGHT

Why do you think the two boys expected Monkey to solve problems for them?

'I will fix this so that each of you gets the same amount of meat,' said Monkey. And with that he took a bite from the larger piece of meat. But once more he noticed that the two pieces were uneven. And no matter how carefully Monkey bit the pieces of meat, one piece always ended up being bigger. Finally there were only two small pieces of meat.

At that point Monkey said, 'It is time for me to take my fee for being your judge. These two tiny pieces of meat will do just fine.' And with that he sent the two hungry, and wiser, boys on their way.

LEARN MORE! READ THESE ARTICLES…
A KOREAN FOLKTALE: THE TIGER IN THE TRAP (VOLUME 5)
MONKEYS (VOLUME 12) • NIGERIA (VOLUME 8)

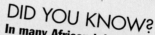

DID YOU KNOW?
In many African tales, the monkey and several other animals are clever and the human beings are usually shown to be foolish.

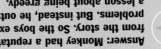

Answer: Monkey had a reputation for being clever, as you see from the story. So the boys expected that he could solve their problems. But instead, he outsmarted them whilst teaching them a lesson about being greedy.

SEARCH LIGHT

Who is
Ntikume?

DID YOU KNOW?
The West African character Ananse
(or Anansi) also appears in Jamaican
tales. This shows how folktales
travelled from Africa with the slave
trade to the West Indies.

Ananse
and the Wisdom Pot

Ananse the spider was far and wide considered to be the wisest of all animals, and many animals came to him with their problems and questions.

After a while, Ananse grew tired of answering so many questions and decided he would have to do something to regain his peace and quiet. So he put all of his wisdom into a giant pot. He strapped the pot to his belly. He planned to carry the pot to a branch of a tall tree where all the animals could go to get their own answers to their questions.

But as he was climbing the tree, the pot kept getting in the way of his legs and slowed him down. Ntikume, one of Ananse's many sons, saw this. He suggested that Ananse strap the pot to his back instead, where it wouldn't be in his way.

When Ananse heard this he was furious. He couldn't **tolerate** the thought that his son should have a better idea than his own. So Ananse grabbed the pot and flung it to the ground, where it shattered into a thousand pieces.

Ever since then, wisdom has been scattered all over the world for many people to find.

LEARN MORE! READ THESE ARTICLES…
AFRICA (VOLUME 8)
AN INUIT TALE: HOW CROW BROUGHT DAYLIGHT TO THE WORLD (VOLUME 5)
SPIDERS (VOLUME 11)

Answer: Ntikume is one of Ananse's many sons.

Yeh-Shen

Once there was a man with a beautiful daughter called Yeh-Shen. **Alas**, before the girl grew up, her father died. So Yeh-Shen was brought up by her stepmother.

Now the stepmother already had a daughter of her own. So the stepmother gave Yeh-Shen all the hardest jobs. Yeh-Shen had no friends other than a golden fish, a carp. Yeh-Shen always shared what she had with her friend the carp.

One day the stepmother discovered Yeh-Shen's secret friend. She caught the fish and cooked it for breakfast. As Yeh-Shen gathered up the bones of the fish, the skeleton told her that it could grant wishes.

Yeh-Shen was eager to go to the Spring Festival. But Yeh-Shen's stepmother refused to let her go. She was afraid that pretty Yeh-Shen would get all the attention and her own daughter would get none. So Yeh-Shen asked the bones for help. As soon as she said the words, she was dressed in a gown of peacock feathers. On her feet were beautiful golden slippers.

At the festival Yeh-Shen danced and danced and had a wonderful time. But when she saw her stepmother approaching, she was frightened and ran away, leaving behind one golden slipper.

The next morning everyone was talking about the beautiful stranger.

DID YOU KNOW?

A 9th-century-AD Chinese version of this classic story is one of the earliest known. There are about 300 different variations of the Cinderella story.

The **magistrate** announced that his son wanted to marry the woman whose foot fitted the slipper. But though many tried, no one's foot would fit.

When the magistrate saw Yeh-Shen, he asked her to try on the slipper. The slipper fitted perfectly. Yeh-Shen and the magistrate's son were married and lived happily together all their lives.

LEARN MORE! READ THESE ARTICLES…
AN ASIAN FOLKTALE: WHO WILL MARRY MOUSIE? (VOLUME 5)
CARP (VOLUME 11) • CHINA (VOLUME 7)

Answer: Instead of a fairy godmother, such as Cinderella had, Yeh-Shen had a magic skeleton (or fish skeleton) to help her.

15

Moni Mekhala
and Ream Eyso

At one time, both the goddess Moni Mekhala and the giant Ream Eyso were studying with the same teacher. This teacher was very wise.

After a few years of teaching them both, the wise teacher decided to hold a contest for her students. She asked them to bring her a full glass of dew the next morning. Whoever brought her a glass full of dew first would win a prize, a magic ball.

Both got up very early and went to gather their glasses of dew.

Ream Eyso was quite pleased with himself. 'Surely my idea of pouring the dew off the leaves is brilliant,' he said.

Moni Mekhala had actually started the night before by laying a scarf on the grass. 'This worked beautifully,' she said as she wrung the scarf out into a cup.

The goddess won the magic ball, and the giant was given a magic axe as a second prize. Ream Eyso was jealous of Moni Mekhala. So he took his axe and threw it at the goddess. It made a terrible rumble as it flew through the air.

Moni Mekhala heard the noise and held up her magic ball. She caused the ball to strike the giant with great, jagged sparks of fire. The fire made him so hot that he dripped large drops of sweat all over the ground.

Even today you can hear the rumble and see the sparks as Ream Eyso's sweat falls to the ground.

LEARN MORE! READ THESE ARTICLES...
ANGKOR WAT (VOLUME 7) • DEW (VOLUME 1)
THUNDER AND LIGHTNING (VOLUME 1)

SEARCH LIGHT

What natural occurrence does this story explain?

DID YOU KNOW?

In North American Indian mythology, a spirit called the Thunderbird watered the Earth. Lightning was believed to flash from its beak, and rolling thunder came from the beating of its wings.

Answer: This story explains the source of thunder, lightning, and rain.

The Poor Man
and the Flask of Oil

About the 8th century, the writer Ibn al-Muqaffa made a famous Arabic translation of the South Asian stories known as tales of Bidpai. The translation was called the *Kalilah wa Dimnah* (after the two jackals in the book's first story, Kalilah and Dimnah). It provided a treasure of tales and parables that would appear throughout Islamic literature. This is one of those well-known tales.

A poor man lived next to a rich man who sold oil for a living. The poor man envied his neighbour's wealth and riches and often talked about them. So the rich man gave the poor man a **flask** of oil as a gift.

The poor man was delighted. 'I could sell the oil,' thought the poor man. 'Then I would have enough money to buy five goats.'

Later he thought some more. 'With five goats,' he said to himself, 'a man would be rich enough to have a wife.' He liked this thought so much he added to it. 'Of course, my wife would be beautiful and give me a fine son.'

But then the poor man had a thought that worried him. 'What if my son is lazy because his father is a wealthy man? What if he refuses to obey me and disgraces me?'

This thought made the poor man so angry that he began stomping around his hut, swinging his staff. 'Why, if my son refuses to obey me, then I'll teach him a lesson. I'll beat him with my **staff**.'

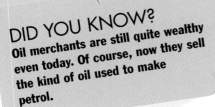

DID YOU KNOW?
Oil merchants are still quite wealthy even today. Of course, now they sell the kind of oil used to make petrol.

SEARCH LIGHT

Why, in the olden days, would a man who sold oil be wealthy?

As the staff swung about, it nudged the flask of oil off its shelf. The flask crashed to the ground and broke, spilling its contents on the dirt. The man looked at the shards of the flask, realizing that his dreams were now just as broken. And once more he was just a poor man living next to a wealthy neighbour.

LEARN MORE! READ THESE ARTICLES...
ASIA (VOLUME 7) • OIL (VOLUME 2)

Answer: Oil has long been used as a fuel for lamps and was very valuable when there wasn't yet any electricity.

19

The Tiger in the Trap

Once there was a traveller. He was just getting ready to stop for the night when he heard a low moaning. He found a tiger trapped in a deep pit.

The tiger saw the man and begged, 'Please free me from this trap, and I will be grateful to you for the rest of my life.'

The traveller agreed and lowered a large branch into the pit for the tiger to climb out. As soon as the tiger was free, he fell upon the man.

'Wait!' said the traveller. 'I thought you were going to be grateful to me.'

'It was men who trapped me,' answered the tiger. 'So a man should suffer for it.'

Just then a **hare** hopped by and asked what was happening. The tiger explained and then asked if the hare agreed with him.

'First I have to see the pit. Where were you?' the hare asked the tiger.

'Down here,' the tiger replied and jumped into the pit.

'Was the branch there too?' asked the hare.

'No,' said the tiger. And so the hare took the branch away.

Then the hare turned to the traveller and told him to be on his way.

The tiger cried out in **dismay** as the man walked off down the trail. 'How could you betray me?'

'I judge each according to his own and not by his fellows,' answered the hare. 'You have the fate you deserve and so does the man.'

LEARN MORE! READ THESE ARTICLES...
KOREAN PENINSULA (VOLUME 7)
A NIGERIAN FOLKTALE: THE MONKEY COURT (VOLUME 5)
TIGER (VOLUME 12)

DID YOU KNOW?

Despite the many stories, tigers seldom eat people. Usually a tiger attacks a person only if the tiger is sick or is unable to hunt its natural prey.

Answer: Other men had trapped the tiger so the tiger thought this man should pay for it.

How Kangaroo
Got His Tail

SEARCH LIGHT

Match up
the animals
with their
descriptions.
Kangaroo Wombat
*sleeps outside
sleeps in a hole
flat head
long tail*

Long ago, before kangaroos had long tails and before wombats had flat heads, the animals played and lived together. Kangaroo and Wombat were great friends and spent every day together. But at night, each one liked to sleep in a different way. Wombat liked to sleep indoors, warm and snug. Kangaroo liked to sleep outdoors, beneath the stars. Each thought his way of sleeping was the best.

Then, one night, a terrible storm cracked open the sky, and harsh winds and rain **scoured** the land. Kangaroo was outside and was miserable in the cold, wet night. He knocked on Wombat's house and called to Wombat to let him come in to warm up. But Wombat thought about the amount of space Kangaroo would take up, so he refused to let him in.

Kangaroo was very angry about being locked out in the storm. He picked up a big rock and dropped it through the roof of Wombat's house.

'There,' Kangaroo shouted. 'Now your house will be damp all the time.'

The rock landed on Wombat's head and flattened his brow. Wombat grabbed a spear and threw it as hard as he could at Kangaroo. The spear pierced the end of Kangaroo's tail.

No matter how hard Kangaroo pulled, the spear wouldn't come out, and his tail just stretched longer and longer.

Since that day, Kangaroo and Wombat have not been friends. Kangaroo still has a big tail and sleeps outside. And Wombat still has a flat head and sleeps in a hole.

Answer: Kangaroo: sleeps outside, long tail
Wombat: sleeps in a hole, flat head

Animal Stories That Teach

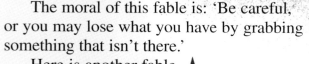

Aesop's fables are animal stories that were told in Greece almost 2,500 years ago. They are stories about animals or birds that speak and act like people. Each of these stories tells us a useful truth about everyday life. These truths are called 'morals'.

One of Aesop's fables is about a greedy dog.

A dog had a piece of meat in his mouth and was carrying it home. On the way, the dog looked into a pond and saw his own reflection. It looked like another dog with a second piece of meat. 'Why should *he* eat such good meat?' thought the dog. 'I want that piece too.'

The dog opened his mouth to grab the other piece of meat, and his piece dropped into the water and disappeared. When the greedy dog saw the meat disappear, he put his tail between his legs and crept away.

The moral of this fable is: 'Be careful, or you may lose what you have by grabbing something that isn't there.'

Here is another fable, about a fox.

SEARCH LIGHT

True or false? The dog lost his meat because he was hungry.

Strolling through the woods one day, a fox saw a juicy bunch of grapes hanging from a high vine.

'Just the thing for a thirsty fox,' he said to himself.

The fox jumped as high as he could, but he could not reach the grapes. He tried again and again. Each time he just missed the tasty-looking fruit. 'Oh well,' he thought. 'Those grapes are probably sour anyway.' And he went away without the grapes.

The term 'sour grapes' comes from this Aesop's fable about the fox. It refers to the attitude some people show when they sneer at something they can't have.

LEARN MORE! READ THESE ARTICLES...
GRAPES (VOLUME 10) • GREECE (VOLUME 6)
MYTHS AND LEGENDS, FOLKTALES AND FABLES (VOLUME 5)

Answer: FALSE. The dog lost his meat because he was greedy.

SEARCH LIGHT

How many
eyes does the
Cyclops have?
a) a million
b) ten
c) one

DID YOU KNOW?
Some scientists think the legend of
Cyclops might have developed when
people found elephant bones and
didn't know what they were. The
elephant skull has a large hole that
looks like a single eye socket.

Odysseus
and the Cyclops

Long ago, the Greek king Odysseus was sailing home from war with his men. Along the way, they stopped at an island where one-eyed man-eating giants called Cyclopes lived.

Odysseus and his men wandered into a cave belonging to the Cyclops Polyphemus. At **twilight** Polyphemus returned with his flocks of sheep. When Polyphemus and all the sheep were inside, he picked up a huge stone and closed the mouth of the cave. Odysseus and his men were trapped!

Polyphemus ate up two of Odysseus' men and fell fast asleep. In the morning he ate two more men and, after blocking the mouth of the cave, went off with his sheep. The stone was too heavy for the men to move. Odysseus, however, thought of a plan. He sharpened the branch of an olive tree.

When Polyphemus came home that night, Odysseus offered him wine. The Cyclops drank it and asked Odysseus' name.

Odysseus answered, 'People call me Nobody.'

'Your gift, Nobody, is that I shall eat you last,' said Polyphemus. And, drunk with wine, he fell fast asleep.

Odysseus then took the great sharp branch and drove it into the sleeping giant's eye, blinding him. When Polyphemus cried out for help, the other Cyclopes shouted, 'Who is hurting you?'

'Nobody,' screamed Polyphemus.

'Well, then you don't need any help from us,' said the other giants.

Meanwhile, Odysseus and each of his men **lashed** together three sheep. Under the middle sheep, each man clung to the **fleece**. Finally everybody was hidden.

Polyphemus did not think of feeling under the bellies of the sheep. And so the men escaped to their ship and continued their long journey home.

LEARN MORE! READ THESE ARTICLES…
GREECE (VOLUME 6) • MYTHS AND LEGENDS, FOLKTALES AND FABLES (VOLUME 5)
SHIPS (VOLUME 2)

The Bearer of the World

Long, long ago, Zeus, the king of the ancient Greek gods, was very angry with Atlas, one of the Titans (the children of Heaven and Earth). He was angry because Atlas had tried to fight with him. So Zeus ordered Atlas to stand forever holding the heavens and the Earth on his shoulders!

Atlas wanted to get rid of his tiresome job. He almost managed this when the Greek hero Hercules came to ask for his help. Hercules was supposed to get three golden apples that were guarded by a dragon in a garden. Atlas agreed to get the apples if Hercules would hold the heavens and the Earth on his shoulders while he was gone.

When Atlas returned, he told Hercules to keep the job. Hercules agreed. But he asked Atlas to hold the world for just a minute while he found a shoulder-pad for himself. As soon as Atlas lifted the world onto his shoulders, Hercules picked up the golden apples and ran away. Some stories say that thunder is Atlas shouting after Hercules to come back. Most pictures of Atlas show him carrying the world.

This is an ancient Greek story. But today, when we want to learn about the world, we look in a book called an 'atlas'. Here we can see the shapes of countries, the rivers that flow in each country, and where the continents are.

LEARN MORE! READ THESE ARTICLES...
GRAVITY (VOLUME 2) • GREECE (VOLUME 6)
A GREEK LEGEND: ODYSSEUS AND THE CYCLOPS (VOLUME 5)

SEARCH LIGHT

Find and correct the mistakes in the following sentence: Hercules agreed to get three golden apples for Atlas if Atlas would hold the heavens and Earth on his shoulders for a while.

DID YOU KNOW?

Atlas is also the name of a range of mountains in north-western Africa. In one story, Atlas was the king of that area. But he was a bad host to the Greek hero Perseus, who showed him the Gorgon's head. Looking at the Gorgon turned men to stone.

Answer: Atlas agreed to get three golden apples for Hercules if Hercules would hold the heavens and Earth on his shoulders for a while.

29

The Golem
of Prague

Many hundreds of years ago there lived many Jewish families in the city of Prague. Although they worked hard, many people in Prague didn't like them. Sometimes Jewish businesses were raided. Sometimes their homes were burned. And sometimes they were killed.

In that time there was a wise rabbi, a great teacher, living in Prague. His name was Rabbi Loew. He knew a way to help his people. He would build a man of clay. He would make the Golem.

Rabbi Loew shaped clay into the form of a man's body. And when he was done, he walked around the clay man seven times, chanting, 'Shanti, Shanti, Dahat, Dahat.' The Golem then opened his eyes and sat up.

'Golem,' said Rabbi Loew. 'I've made you so you can help and protect my people.' The Golem nodded.

'Every day I'll tell you what to do,' continued Rabbi Loew.

At first the Golem was a great gift to the Jewish families of Prague. He helped them in their work and protected them. But the Golem wanted more. So Rabbi Loew taught him to read. But reading about people made him want even more. He wanted to be human.

Rabbi Loew couldn't make the Golem human. The Golem became angry and began to attack the people he had earlier helped. He became a monster.

Rabbi Loew had no choice but to chase the Golem from Prague. No one knows what happened to the Golem. And no one knows where he is today.

LEARN MORE! READ THESE ARTICLES...
DRAGONS: BEASTS OF FIRE AND MIST (VOLUME 5)
JUDAISM (VOLUME 5) • PRAGUE (VOLUME 6)

DID YOU KNOW?
Modern-day horror films have used the idea of man-made monsters. Perhaps most famous are the various versions of the monster movie *Frankenstein.*

SEARCH LIGHT

The golem
was a
a) clay beast.
b) clay man.
c) clay toy.

Answer: b) clay man.

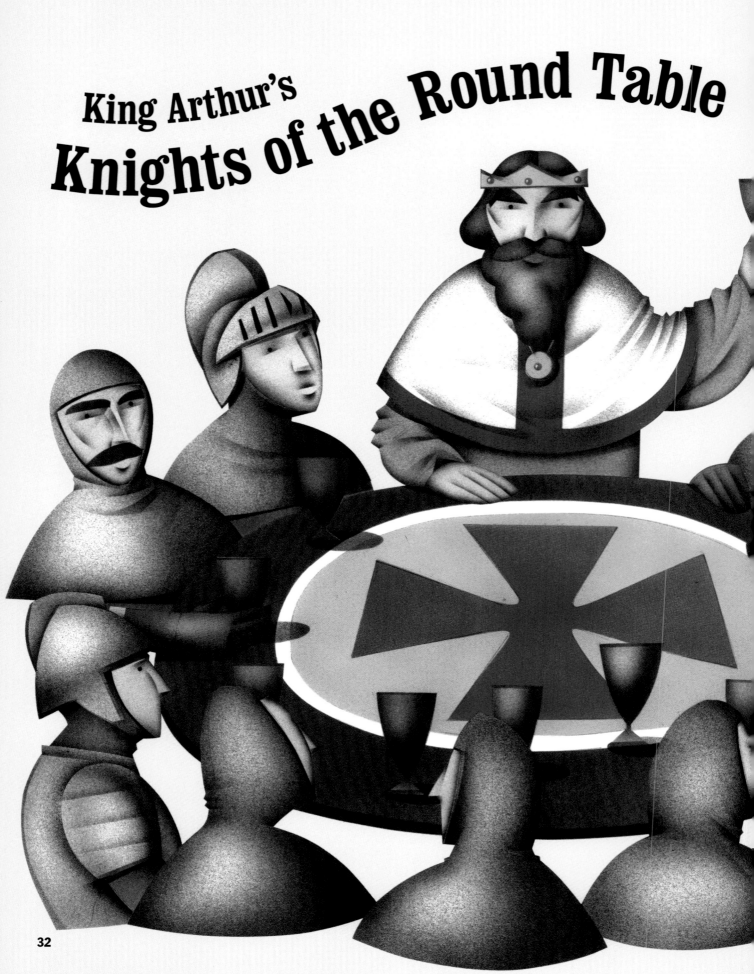

King Arthur's
Knights of the Round Table

It is said that, long ago, the British people needed a king. One day, the legend goes, a rock appeared with a sword caught in it.

A sign said: 'Whoever Can Pull This Sword from This Rock Will Be Rightful King of the Britons.'

The strongest men in the kingdom tried to pull the sword out of the rock. It would not move. Then along came a young boy called Arthur. He had not heard about the sword in the rock. Thinking he would borrow the sword for his stepbrother, who had gone off to war, Arthur stepped up to the rock. He pulled. The sword slid out easily.

Merlin the magician had placed the sword in the rock. He had kept it there by magic. Only Arthur could remove it. The sword was called Excalibur. Merlin had been Arthur's teacher. He knew that Arthur would be the best king for Britain.

As king, Arthur needed people to help him rule wisely. He decided he would ask the strongest and bravest men to help him. He sent messengers to look for these strong and brave men.

Many men came to help Arthur. He asked them to promise to be fair, to keep their word and to protect the weak. They became Arthur's Knights of the Round Table. Lancelot would become the greatest of all the Knights of the Round Table. But Arthur made the table round for a reason. It meant that everyone seated was equal there, and no one could sit at the 'head' of the table.

King Arthur's legend also says that if Britain is ever in danger, he will come back and save the people once again.

LEARN MORE! READ THESE ARTICLES...
ELIZABETH I (VOLUME 4) • ENGLAND (VOLUME 6)
MYTHS AND LEGENDS, FOLKTALES AND FABLES (VOLUME 5)

SEARCH LIGHT

Find and correct the mistake in the following sentence: The name of Arthur's famous sword was Lancelot.

DID YOU KNOW?
Although the Arthur story is a legend, there might really have been a 6th-century military leader who led the British against invaders.

Answer: The name of Arthur's famous sword was Excalibur.
(Lancelot was a famous Knight of the Round Table.)

33

How Crow Brought Daylight to the World

There was a time when the world of the north was always in darkness. The people wished for light and Crow told them he had seen daylight on one of his many travels.

'Please bring us some daylight,' the people begged Crow.

Crow flew for many miles. Just when he thought he couldn't fly any more, he saw daylight ahead of him.

When he reached daylight, he landed in a tree to rest. While Crow was resting, the chief's daughter came along. Crow turned himself into a speck of dust and landed on the girl's **parka**. Then Crow heard a baby crying.

'What's wrong?' the girl asked her young brother.

Crow drifted into the baby's ear and whispered: 'Tell her you want a ball of daylight to play with.'

The chief's daughter tied a piece of string to a ball of daylight and gave it to her brother to play with. When the girl carried her brother and the ball of daylight outside, Crow turned back into a bird, grabbed the ball by its string and flew away.

When he arrived home, the people were overjoyed. 'We have daylight!' they cheered. 'We can see the whole world.'

But Crow warned them: 'It is just a small ball of daylight. It will need to rest every now and then, so you won't have daylight for the whole year.'

And that is why the people of the frozen north have half a year of daylight and half a year of darkness.

LEARN MORE! READ THESE ARTICLES…
AKLAVIK (VOLUME 9) • BIRDS (VOLUME 11) • SOLAR SYSTEM (VOLUME 2)

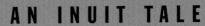

SEARCH LIGHT

Fill in the gap: This story explains why there is daylight for only _____ the year in the far north.

DID YOU KNOW?
Crow is a popular figure because of his wisdom. He appears in many Native American myths.

Why Possum's Tail Is Bare

Possum once had a bushy tail covered with thick, glossy fur. In conversation, he always managed to mention his tail: 'When I was brushing my beautiful tail yesterday, you'll never guess what I saw...'

The other animals were tired of hearing about Possum's tail. But Rabbit said: 'Don't worry, I have a plan.'

The next day Rabbit announced that there was going to be a grand dance. 'We'll want to do something special with your tail,' he said to Possum.

'First,' said Rabbit, 'we need to wash and comb your tail.'

So they dipped Possum's tail in the river, and then Rabbit pulled a pine cone through Possum's tail fur.

'Ouch!' cried Possum. 'You're hurting me.'

'I can stop if you want me to,' replied Rabbit.

'No, no,' said Possum. 'Keep working on my tail.'

So Rabbit kept pulling the pine cone sharply over Possum's tail.

'Now we'll just wrap your tail in this red ribbon,' Rabbit told him.

SEARCH LIGHT

This story
explains
why possums
a) play dead.
b) climb trees.
c) carry their babies.

Possum was so excited. As soon as he reached the dance, he untied the ribbon. And as he did so, all the other animals started to laugh.

'What's so funny?' shouted Possum. Then he looked at his tail. It was as bare and smooth as Snake's back. Rabbit had pulled all the fur off Possum's tail!

'Oh, oh!' wailed Possum and fainted on his back.

And that's why, when you see Possum today, his tail is bare, and if you scare him he rolls over onto his back.

LEARN MORE! READ THESE ARTICLES...
AMERICAN INDIANS (VOLUME 4)
AN AUSTRALIAN TALE: HOW KANGAROO GOT HIS TAIL (VOLUME 5)
OPOSSUMS (VOLUME 12)

DID YOU KNOW?
'Possum' is a shortened form of 'opossum', the full name of this American animal. It's a member of the marsupial family, as are the kangaroos and koalas of Australia.

DID YOU KNOW?
The legend of Paul Bunyan may have come from stories that real lumberjacks told around the fire on cold evenings.

The Tale of a Lumberjack

If somebody told you that a giant woodsman had created a 160 kilometre-long inlet to float logs to a mill, would you believe it? Probably not, but it makes a good story.

Stories like that are called 'tall tales', and an imaginary giant lumberjack named Paul Bunyan figures in many American tall tales. A lumberjack is a man who earns his living by cutting down trees. Paul was so big and powerful that he could make hills, lakes, and rivers whenever he wanted to. In fact, he's supposed to have created the Grand Canyon and the Great Lakes.

Paul Bunyan was so big that when he sneezed, a whole hillside of pine trees would fall over. Being such a large man, Paul would get very hungry. He was especially fond of pancakes. The frying pan for making them was so big that people would skate around it with slabs of bacon tied to their feet to grease it.

Paul had a famous helper that he found during the 'blue winter'. People called it the 'blue winter' because the snow that fell was all blue! One night Paul heard an animal crying. When he looked outside, he saw a pair of silky blue ears sticking out of the snow. Paul pulled and pulled. Out of the blue snow came a baby blue ox!

Paul took the ox home with him and named it Babe. When Babe grew up, he was nearly as big as a small mountain.

One story tells of a road with so many curves in it that people didn't know whether they were coming or going. Paul laughed and picked up one end of the road and tied it to Babe. Babe tugged and pulled all the curves out of the road.

LEARN MORE! READ THESE ARTICLES…
ATLAS: THE BEARER OF THE WORLD (VOLUME 5)
GRAND CANYON (VOLUME 9) • GREAT LAKES (VOLUME 9)

Answer: FALSE. As far as anyone knows there never was an actual lumberjack named Paul Bunyan.

Rabbit Throws Away His Sandal

Rabbit was the wisest of all the animals, and so he was their mayor. Although he was a good leader, he wasn't well liked because he used his wits to play tricks on the other animals.

One morning all the animals decided they would get rid of Rabbit and his tricks. They gathered outside of Rabbit's burrow, planning to grab him and tear him to pieces as soon as he came out.

But Rabbit heard them grumbling. He called back, 'I'll be out as soon as I find my sandals.'

It was still dark as the Sun had yet to rise. The animals all began to shout, 'Rabbit, hurry up. We need your help.'

Rabbit called back, 'I've found one sandal, but it's broken and it'll take time to fix it.'

DID YOU KNOW?

Rabbits appear in the folktales of several different cultures. For instance the Brer ('Brother') Rabbit of African American tales grew out of an African character, Hare. Both are clever, like Rabbit in this Mayan story from Central America.

SEARCH LIGHT

Which animal is not in the story?
a) dog
b) skunk
c) snake

Jaguar, who was quite impatient, said, 'Throw it out here and I'll fix it while you look for the other sandal.'

Jaguar grabbed the object that flew out of the burrow and tossed it into bushes.

After a while, Skunk said, 'What's keeping you, Rabbit?' But no one answered.

Then Vulture said, 'Snake, slither into that hole and see what's keeping Rabbit.'

Snake did just that. But he could see very quickly that he was alone in the burrow. 'There's no one here. Rabbit's disappeared.'

Then from the bushes everyone heard Rabbit laugh. They realized he had tricked them once again. They had been so eager waiting for Rabbit that no one noticed he had thrown himself out instead of his sandal.

LEARN MORE! READ THESE ARTICLES...
A CHEROKEE STORY: WHY POSSUM'S TAIL IS BARE (VOLUME 5)
GUATEMALA (VOLUME 9) • MAYAN CIVILIZATION (VOLUME 4)

Answer: a) dog

Belief in a Higher Power

There are many people in the world who believe in a god or gods. Others do not use the word 'god' but still believe that there are other, greater forces at work in their lives. The way groups of people worship these forces or their gods forms what we call a 'religion'.

Many different religions are practised around the world. Major religions today include Christianity, Islam, Judaism, Hinduism, Daoism, Sikhism, and Buddhism. Most religions try to answer the same basic questions: How was the world created? What is the meaning of human life? Why do people die and what happens afterward? Why is there evil? How should people behave?

Worshippers in Nepal celebrate Buddha Jayanti, honouring the Buddha's birth, death, and Enlightenment.
© Macduff Everton/Corbis

Many religions have buildings set aside for worship. In these temples, cathedrals, mosques, and churches, activities such as prayer, **sacrifice**, and other forms of worship take place.

At different times in history, followers of one religion have tried to make others believe in that religion. Sometimes this was done by peaceful means. Often, however, it was done by force - sometimes by 'holy wars'.

For instance, between 1095 and 1292, European Christians led a number of **crusades** against Muslims. In these crusades Christians tried to take control of the holy city of Jerusalem and other places they associated with the life of Jesus Christ. Muslims also carried out holy wars, or jihads. At various times Muslims spread into much of the Middle East and parts of Europe and Asia.

Most religions, however, encourage their followers to live peacefully with people of other religions. And, in fact, they share many **aspects** in common. These include **rituals** to perform, prayers to recite, places to visit or avoid, days that are holy, holy books to read and study, and leaders to follow.

LEARN MORE! READ THESE ARTICLES...
CHARLEMAGNE (VOLUME 4) • GOD (VOLUME 5) • MONASTICISM (VOLUME 5)

Roman Catholics worship together in a service called 'mass'. Here the mass is being led by Pope John Paul II, world leader of the church, in Saint Peter's Basilica in Rome, Italy.
© Vittoriano Rastelli/Corbis

SEARCH LIGHT

True or false? All religions have a single god.

Answer: FALSE. Some religions have one god. But others have many gods, and some have no god at all.

One World, Many Beliefs

How did the universe start? How did life on Earth begin?

For thousands of years people have searched for the answers to such questions. Some people believe that science will solve the mysteries. But in the earliest times, science could not explain natural events such as earthquakes and storms, day and night, and life and death. People believed that these things were the work of beings greater and more powerful than humans: the gods.

Stained-glass image showing a Christian artist's idea of God the Father, with angels.
© Royalty-Free/Corbis

Today many people still seek an understanding of life through the worship of a god or gods. They often feel that their faith helps them live better lives.

Some religions, such as Judaism, Christianity, and Islam, teach that there is only one God, a **supreme** being who made the universe and controls the world. This is called 'monotheism', from the Greek words for 'one' and 'God'. The worship of several powerful gods is called 'polytheism', because 'poly' means 'many'. Ancient Greeks and Romans believed in many gods, whom we know today from ancient **myths** and art.

People from different places and cultures have their own names for their gods. The God of the ancient Jews was called Yahweh. Muslims use the Arabic word for God, Allah. Hindus believe in a large number of gods and goddesses (female gods). Each of them has a different personality and controls a different **aspect** of life. They believe these gods are forms of one supreme god. One popular Hindu god is the elephant-headed Ganesha. Many Hindus appeal to Ganesha when they begin an important new project.

The behaviour of a god can vary from religion to religion. Some religions may see their god or gods as cruel and unforgiving. Others consider their god to be kind and merciful. But all gods play a part in helping people understand their world.

DID YOU KNOW?
Not only did the ancient Egyptians believe in a large family of gods, but they also believed that their pharaoh, or king, was a god.

LEARN MORE! READ THESE ARTICLES...
MYTHS AND LEGENDS, FOLKTALES AND FABLES (VOLUME 5) • RELIGION (VOLUME 5)
UNIVERSE (VOLUME 2)

SEARCH LIGHT

Fill in the gap: The Hindu god of successful beginnings is _____ .

In many world religions, worshippers like this woman in Hong Kong burn incense to honour their gods.

© Royalty-Free/Corbis

Answer: The Hindu god of successful beginnings is Ganesha.

A Life Apart

Most major religions have a tradition of monasticism. Monasticism comes from the Greek word for 'living alone'. So monks - men who practice monasticism - are people who choose to live apart from society. This allows them to devote themselves to a religious life. Women who choose this way of life are called 'nuns'.

Not all monks and nuns live entirely by themselves. Many live in communities with other monks or nuns. These community homes are usually called 'monasteries' or, for nuns, 'convents'. Life in a religious community generally focuses on prayer, **meditation**, and religious works. Monks and nuns may concentrate on building a personal relationship with God. They may work to purify their thought and reach spiritual perfection.

Some monks do live all by themselves as **hermits**. And some wander from place to place their entire lives. But whether they live in a community or by themselves, all monks and nuns give up certain of life's pleasures. Many don't own property or have any money. Others force themselves to face certain challenges, such as **fasting** or other physical discomforts.

Monks and nuns choose to live apart so that they won't be distracted by life. Usually, they are unmarried, since having a family requires great dedication and time. The monastic life allows people to focus as much of themselves as possible on God and on the **salvation** their religion promises.

Many monks and nuns do still take part in the world around them. For example, they may serve as teachers, social workers, missionaries, or nurses. In earlier times monks were often among the few people who could read and write. So they're responsible for having preserved much of written world history and culture.

LEARN MORE! READ THESE ARTICLES...
DALAI LAMA (VOLUME 5) • ROMAN CATHOLICISM (VOLUME 5)
VIVEKANANDA (VOLUME 5)

Answer: FALSE. Almost all the world's major religions have some tradition of monasticism.

Eternal Battle of Good and Evil

Over 2,700 years ago, a man named Zoroaster lived in Persia (modern Iran). At that time people worshipped many gods. Zoroaster's beliefs opposed this way of thinking.

Zoroaster denied the power of lesser gods and honoured one god as supreme - Ahura Mazda, also called Ormazd. The power of evil he named Ahriman. Zoroaster preached that a struggle between the two resulted in the creation of the world. Since its creation, the whole world has been involved in the battle between good and evil, light and darkness. Each human being struggles between good and evil. After a person dies, the soul crosses a bridge and passes into either heaven or hell.

Zoroastrians also believe that the history of the world is a vast drama divided into four periods of 3,000 years each. At the end of the first 3,000 years, the creation of the world takes place. At the end of the second, Ahriman arrives to corrupt the creation. In the third period, he triumphs but finds himself trapped in creation and doomed to cause his own destruction. In the fourth period, religion comes to Earth through the birth of Zoroaster.

Each 1,000 years thereafter, a new **prophet** will appear. The last of these will bring the final judgment and a new world.

Islamic armies invaded Iran about 1,400 years ago. Eventually, most Zoroastrians left Iran and settled in India around Bombay (now called Mumbai). These people came to be known as Parsis. The Parsis grew into a rich and highly educated community.

The holy book of the Zoroastrians is the *Avesta*. The central feature of their temples is a sacred fire that burns night and day and is never allowed to die out.

SEARCH LIGHT

Who represents good in Zoroastrianism, Ahura Mazda or Ahriman?

LEARN MORE! READ THESE ARTICLES...
GOD (VOLUME 5) • IRAN (VOLUME 7) • RELIGION (VOLUME 5)

DID YOU KNOW?
Zoroaster is sometimes credited with having created the practice of astrology. Astrologers 'read' the heavens in order to predict events and determine people's characters.

Between the ages of 7 and 11, children are initiated into the Zoroastrian religion in a ceremony called *navjote*. Here, priests oversee this young Parsi (Indian Zoroastrian) boy's *navjote*.
© Tim Page/Corbis

Answer: Ahura Mazda represents good in Zoroastrianism.

Religion of Israel

The Jews call themselves 'Israel', which in Hebrew means 'the people chosen by God'. According to Jewish holy writings, the one God promised Abraham, the father of all Jews: 'I will make of thee a great nation.' In return, that nation, Israel, was to obey God forever.

Later, when the people of Israel were enslaved in Egypt, a leader named Moses freed them and led the Jews to a new home. While going there, they made an agreement with God in the form of the **commandments**, God's laws. The commandments remind the Jewish people of their responsibilities to God and to each other.

Lighting the menorah in celebration of the Jewish festival of Hanukkah.
© Richard T. Nowitz/Corbis

All of this is written in the Hebrew Bible (known as the Old Testament to Christians). The most important section of the Hebrew Bible is the Torah - also called the Five Books of Moses, or Pentateuch. The Torah contains the religious ideas, history, ceremonies, and **rituals** of Judaism.

When a Jewish boy turns 13, he must read from the Torah in public. This makes him a Bar Mitzvah, or 'son of the commandment'. Girls celebrate their Bas Mitzvah, or Bat Mitzvah, which takes place after their 12th birthday.

Jews worship in synagogues, where services include the reading of the Scriptures, praying, and offering blessings and thanks to God. Important Jewish holidays are Purim, Rosh Hoshanah, and Hanukkah. The festival of Passover begins with a religious meal.

Today there are different groups within Judaism. **Orthodox** Jews dress, eat, live, and worship very much like their ancestors did hundreds of years ago. **Conservative** Jews worship much like Orthodox Jews but live by more relaxed rules. Reform Jews worship in more modern ways, with even fewer rules about how they live their daily lives.

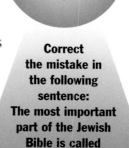

SEARCH LIGHT

Correct the mistake in the following sentence: The most important part of the Jewish Bible is called the Bat Mitzvah.

LEARN MORE! READ THESE ARTICLES...
BIBLE (VOLUME 5) • ISRAEL (VOLUME 7)
A JEWISH LEGEND: THE GOLEM OF PRAGUE (VOLUME 5)

Young Jewish boys all over the world celebrate their Bar Mitzvah. This young man carries the Torah at the Western Wall in Jerusalem as part of his celebration.
© Richard T. Nowitz/Corbis

DID YOU KNOW?
Many Jews 'keep kosher', which means they observe special laws about the food they eat. There are strict rules for how food is prepared and whether certain foods can be eaten in combination or at all.

Answer: The most important part of the Jewish Bible is called the Torah.

Father of
Many Nations

The first book of the Bible tells the story of Abraham. This honoured leader is important in the major religious **traditions** of the Jews, Christians, and Muslims.

According to the account in the Bible, God came to Abraham one day and told him: 'I will make of thee a great nation.' God commanded him to leave his home in Mesopotamia (modern Iraq) for an unknown land, which would belong to Abraham and his descendants.

At the age of 75, Abraham started on this journey, bringing his wife, Sarah, and some other companions. They reached the '**Promised Land**', then known as Canaan, in what is now Israel.

SEARCH LIGHT

How old was Abraham when he went on his journey to Canaan?
a) 175
b) 100
c) 75

Because Abraham and Sarah were so old when they settled there, they thought they couldn't have children. So Sarah gave Abraham her slave Hagar to have a child with, and Hagar gave birth to a son, Ishmael. But God had promised Abraham and Sarah their own child. When Abraham was 100 years old and Sarah was 90, their son, Isaac, was born. Sarah later sent Hagar and Ishmael away to live in the desert. Many consider Ishmael the first of the Arab people.

God tested Abraham by ordering him to kill Isaac as a sacrifice. Abraham was upset, but he was ready to obey. God stopped Abraham, however, and, because of his obedience, blessed him and his descendants. Isaac inherited the Promised Land after his father died and is considered to be the father of the Jewish people.

Abraham died when he was 175 years old and was buried next to Sarah. Abraham is still respected and honoured by Christians, Jews, and Muslims. They honour him as the father of their religion and as a great **prophet**.

DID YOU KNOW?
Islamic tradition says that Abraham, assisted by his son Ishmael, built the Kaaba, the holiest of Muslim shrines, in the centre of the Great Mosque in Mecca, Saudi Arabia.

LEARN MORE! READ THESE ARTICLES...
BIBLE (VOLUME 5) • ISLAM (VOLUME 5) • ISRAEL (VOLUME 7)

Yahweh's Messenger

According to the Jewish Bible, the Hebrew people first went to Egypt in search of food during a great **famine**. Eventually, the Egyptians came to fear the Hebrews and enslaved them. At one point the pharaoh, the ruler of Egypt, ordered that all newborn male Hebrews be killed. Moses was born about this time, more than 3,000 years ago.

According to the Bible, Moses' parents set him afloat on the Nile River in a reed basket. The pharaoh's daughter found the child while she was bathing. Moses thus grew up in the Egyptian court. One day he learned that he was a Hebrew. He went out to visit his people and saw the hard life they led. Moses saw an Egyptian **overseer** beating a Hebrew slave, and he killed the overseer. He realized that he would have to flee.

Moses found shelter with a priest, married the priest's daughter, and became a shepherd. While looking after the flock, Moses heard God for the first time. God spoke to him from a burning bush on Mount Sinai, identifying himself as Yahweh. He told Moses to go back to Egypt and demand that the pharaoh set the Hebrews free.

Moses tried. But when the pharaoh refused, Yahweh punished the Egyptians with ten plagues. The tenth took the life of the pharaoh's eldest son, so the pharaoh ordered the Hebrews to leave.

Through much hardship, Moses led his people toward the Promised Land of Canaan. At Mount Sinai, Yahweh told Moses to go up the mountain. There Moses received the Ten **Commandments**. These laws and others told the Hebrews how to live. They became part of the Torah, the first five books of the Bible, and bound Jews to God.

LEARN MORE! READ THESE ARTICLES...
BIBLE (VOLUME 5) • EGYPT (VOLUME 7)
JUDAISM (VOLUME 5)

SEARCH LIGHT

True or false? Moses grew up in the Egyptian court of the pharaoh.

DID YOU KNOW?
The Bible says that as Moses and the Hebrews fled the Egyptian soldiers chasing them, they came to a body of water believed to be the Red Sea. Yahweh created a dry path for the Hebrews to cross, but he drowned the Egyptian soldiers who followed.

The famous artist Michelangelo created this sculpture of Moses, the founder of the religious community of Israel.
© John Heseltine/Corbis

Following Jesus Christ

SEARCH LIGHT

Christians celebrate Christmas to honour Jesus Christ's
a) birth.
b) death.
c) resurrection.

More than two billion people around the world follow the teachings of Jesus Christ. They call themselves Christians. And their religion, Christianity, is the world's most widespread religion.

Christianity developed from Judaism about 2,000 years ago. Over the years it has split into many groups. This is because, at various times, Christians disagreed among themselves about some of their beliefs. The major branches of Christianity include the Roman Catholic church, Protestant churches, and the Eastern Orthodox church.

Despite the divisions, there are many things these groups agree on. They all have the same holy book, the Bible. The Christian Bible is divided into the Old Testament and the New Testament, which is about the life and teachings of Jesus Christ. Nearly all Christian churches have leaders, or clergy. In different churches they may be called priests, ministers, or pastors, among other titles. Clergy give their church members guidance and perform official duties at services of **worship**.

Most Christians believe in the Trinity as well. The word comes from Latin and means 'three'. It describes the three individual **aspects** of the one God. The three are: God the Father, who created everything; God the Son (Jesus Christ), who died to save humankind; and God the Holy Spirit, who inspires people's thoughts and actions.

And all Christians celebrate certain holy days. Christmas marks the birth of Jesus, and Easter honours Jesus' resurrection, when he rose from the dead. The Friday before Easter is called Good Friday. It is the anniversary of Jesus' death.

LEARN MORE! READ THESE ARTICLES...
CHARLEMAGNE (VOLUME 4) • JESUS CHRIST (VOLUME 5)
JUDAISM (VOLUME 5)

DID YOU KNOW?
Although Christianity is widespread today, its followers were pursued and tormented in the religion's early days. Sometimes they were killed if they were discovered to be Christians.

Answer: a) birth.

The Son of God

Almost everything we know about Jesus Christ comes from the Christian Bible. Jesus was a Jew, born to Mary more than 2,000 years ago in Bethlehem. Christians believe that Jesus was the son of God. The New Testament **Gospels** of the Christian Bible tell the story of Jesus' life and teachings.

Jesus grew up in Nazareth, in what is now Israel. When he was 12 his parents took him to Jerusalem for the feast of Passover. Suddenly they discovered that he was missing. They finally found Jesus talking in the Temple with the learned men, who were amazed at how wise he was.

Like his earthly father, Joseph, he became a carpenter. When Jesus was about 30 years old, he began **preaching** about God. He is also said to have begun performing miracles. In one miracle Jesus fed 5,000 people with just five loaves of bread and two fish.

Jesus was kind to the poor and the sick. He was also kind to people who were disliked by others. He taught that all people should love each another just as they love their families and themselves. Jesus taught about the kingdom of God. Some people thought this meant that Jesus would try to rule a kingdom here on earth. The rulers of the land thought Jesus might try to seize power from them. So at age 33 Jesus was arrested, killed on a cross, and buried. But visitors to his tomb found it empty.

According to the Gospels, Jesus rose from the dead and was taken back up to heaven. First, however, he appeared many times to his followers. His followers became known as Christians, and their religion is called Christianity. They see Jesus' death as a **sacrifice** for all people.

Mosaic picture of Jesus Christ in the cathedral in Cefalù, Sicily, Italy.
© Mimmo Jodice/Corbis

SEARCH LIGHT

Fill in the gap: Jesus taught that people should love each other as much as they love their families and _____.

DID YOU KNOW?
'Christ' was originally a title that came from the Greek word *christos*. *Christos* is a translation from the Hebrew term *meshiah* (or Messiah), meaning 'the anointed one', and refers to the king whom the Jews expected to come.

LEARN MORE! READ THESE ARTICLES...
BUDDHA (VOLUME 5) • CHRISTIANITY (VOLUME 5)
JERUSALEM (VOLUME 7)

This stained-glass window in a church in Palo Alto, California, U.S., shows one of Jesus' miracles. This and other major events from Jesus' life are often subjects of Christian art.
© Steve Skjold/Photo Edit

Answer: Jesus taught that people should love each other as much as they love their families and themselves.

Mother of Jesus

Christians worldwide honour Mary, the mother of Jesus. She is known as Saint Mary and the Virgin Mary. But not much is known about Mary's life. What we do know comes from the New Testament of the Christian Bible.

The Bible first mentions Mary as a young girl living in Nazareth, a town north of Jerusalem in Palestine (now in Israel). She was engaged to

A Pietà (image of the Virgin Mary and the dead Christ), by Luis de Morales.
© Archivo Iconografico, S.A./Corbis

marry Joseph, a local carpenter. One day an angel came to her and told her that she had been chosen to give birth to God's son. Later Mary gave birth to Jesus. King Herod heard that a newborn baby would one day become king of the Jews in Herod's own kingdom. Herod ordered all babies under the age of 2 to be killed. Joseph was warned by an angel in a dream, and he fled with Mary and Jesus to Egypt.

Mary appears again at the wedding at Cana, where Jesus performed his first miracle. She was also one of the few followers who did not run away in fear when Jesus Christ died on the cross. The New Testament Book of John describes how Jesus spoke to John and to Mary from the cross, telling them to look after each other. After that, Mary is mentioned as one of the people who devoted themselves to prayer after Jesus rose to heaven. She also took part in the early growth of the church.

But over the centuries, the mother of Jesus has become recognized as a holy person second only to Jesus in the Roman Catholic, Eastern Orthodox, and other churches. Her position has also influenced the lives of women in Christian cultures.

LEARN MORE! READ THESE ARTICLES...
ISRAEL (VOLUME 7) • JESUS CHRIST (VOLUME 5)
MOTHER TERESA (VOLUME 4)

SEARCH LIGHT

True or false? Saint Mary is Jesus' mother.

Mary, often called the Madonna ('Lady'), has been a favourite subject of artists for centuries. Images of Mary and the baby Jesus are a frequent theme, as in Fra Angelico's 'Madonna of Humility', seen here.
© Francis G. Mayer/Corbis

Answer: TRUE.

The Bible was one of the first books printed by
Johannes Gutenberg on the first printing press. This
is one of the few remaining copies.
© David Young-Wolff/Photo Edit

Jewish and Christian Scriptures

Jews and Christians call their scriptures, or holy books, the Bible. But their Bibles are not the same. What Jews call the Bible forms what Christians call the Old Testament. The Christian Bible also contains the New Testament. Both the Old Testament and the New are collections of shorter sections called 'books'.

© CLEO Photography/Photo Edit © Richard T. Nowitz/Corbis

The Jewish Bible tells the history of Israel. It is grouped into three sections: the Law, the Prophets, and the Writings.

The first five books, the Law, are

(Left) Family shares the Bible. (Right) Torah scrolls in the main synagogue in Jerusalem.

also known to Jews as the Torah. The Law describes how the world and people came to be and how Israel was founded. It contains the story of Moses, the Ten Commandments (instructions for life and worship), and other teachings. The section called the Prophets contains the later history of Israel as well as messages passed from God to the Jewish people. The Writings include history, songs and hymns, **psalms**, poetry, stories, and wise sayings.

The New Testament of Christianity tells the story of Jesus Christ and his followers. It is shorter than the Old Testament. There are four sections in the New Testament: the Gospels, the Acts, the Epistles, and Revelation.

The Gospels describe Christ's life, death, and resurrection (raising from the dead). In the Acts of the Apostles, the story and teachings of Jesus' disciples, or followers, are told. The Epistles are letters that various leaders of the early Christian church wrote. The Book of Revelation talks about the end of the world and the events that will take place before the end comes.

None of the original Bible documents still exist. The Bible **texts** are copies of copies that were handed down over many generations.

LEARN MORE! READ THESE ARTICLES...
CHRISTIANITY (VOLUME 5) • ISRAEL (VOLUME 7) • PRINTING (VOLUME 2)

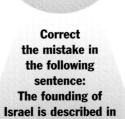

SEARCH LIGHT

Correct the mistake in the following sentence: The founding of Israel is described in the New Testament.

Answer: The founding of Israel is described in the Old Testament.

The Religion of Muhammad

SEARCH LIGHT

Which of the following is not one of the five Pillars of Islam?
a) fasting
b) prayer
c) faith
d) pilgrimage
e) singing
f) giving to the poor

Islam is a major world religion. It was founded in Arabia about 1,400 years ago by a man called Muhammad. Followers of Islam are called Muslims. There are more than a billion Muslims in the world.

Muslims believe that the archangel Gabriel brought Muhammad many messages from God (Allah in Arabic). Most people in Arabia at that time believed in many gods. But the messages told Muhammad that there was only one God. Muslims believe Muhammad was the last of God's prophets, in a line that began with Adam and continued through Abraham, Moses, and Jesus.

The messages to Muhammad were collected in a book called the Koran, or Qur'an. The Koran says that God is stern but forgiving and asks everyone to worship only him. Muslims believe that when they die, they are judged according to their actions.

Palestinian Muslim women pray during Ramadan outside the Dome of the Rock, in Jerusalem.
© AFP/Corbis

Islam has five duties that every Muslim should perform. These five Pillars of Islam instruct Muslims to make known their faith in God, pray daily, give to the poor, **fast,** and make a **pilgrimage** to the holy city of Mecca once during their lifetime if possible.

A Muslim must pray five times a day, either alone or with others in a mosque, the Muslim place of worship. Special group prayers are said in mosques every Friday. Fasting takes place during Ramadan, the holy month during which God is said to have revealed the Koran. During fasting, Muslims may not eat or drink between sunrise and sunset.

Mecca is the holy city of Islam where Muhammad was born and where Abraham built a shrine called the Kaaba. Only Muslims may enter Mecca. The yearly pilgrimage to Mecca is called the *hajj* and is celebrated in the festival of Id al-Adha.

LEARN MORE! READ THESE ARTICLES...
KORAN (VOLUME 5) • MECCA, SAUDI ARABIA (VOLUME 7) • MUHAMMAD (VOLUME 5)

Islam has spread throughout the world, as Muhammad had intended. These Muslims are praying together in a mosque in Sarajevo, in Bosnia and Herzegovina.
© Dean Conger/Corbis

DID YOU KNOW?

Medina, in Saudi Arabia, is celebrated as the first Muslim community. From there, Islam spread throughout Arabia. Only Muslims are allowed to enter the city.

SEARCH LIGHT

Fill in
the gap:
The messages
Muhammad received
from God were
recorded in the
_____.

Islam's Prophet

Muhammad was born in Mecca about 1,400 years ago. During his life he established Islam, one of the world's major religions.

Mecca was a **prosperous** and important centre of trade. Muhammad was a merchant and married a wealthy widow. When he was older, he spent many nights praying in a cave in a hill near Mecca. Muslims believe that on one such night he was visited by the archangel Gabriel, who brought him God's message.

Muhammad believed that God wanted him to deliver God's teachings to the Arab people. These teachings are recorded in Islam's holy book, the Koran. His family and friends accepted Muhammad as the last of a series of **prophets** of God that began with Adam and continued through Abraham, Moses, and Jesus. He then began to preach publicly in Mecca. His religion came to be called Islam, which means 'submission to God'. The believers were called Muslims, which means 'those who have submitted'.

Muhammad said that there was only one God, called Allah in the Arabic language. At that time most Arabs worshipped many different gods. Some people disliked Muhammad's idea and planned to kill him, so he moved to the city of Medina. In his new home he began **converting** people to Islam. After fighting a war with his enemies, Muhammad returned to Mecca and convinced everyone there to become Muslims. Many Arabs then became Muslims, and gradually Muhammad became the leader of Arabia.

Eventually, Islam split into different branches. All Muslims, however, look upon Muhammad as an example of an ideal of human life. They honour three cities connected with him: Mecca (his birthplace), Medina (the first Muslim community), and Jerusalem (which he supposedly visited on a journey to heaven).

LEARN MORE! READ THESE ARTICLES...
GOD (VOLUME 5) • ISLAM (VOLUME 5) • MECCA (VOLUME 7)

The shrine known as the Kaaba, in the holy city of Mecca, is considered by Muslims to be the holiest place on Earth. The yearly *hajj* (or pilgrimage to Mecca) is undertaken by over a million worshippers. Daily prayers are said in the direction of Mecca and the Kaaba.
© AFP/Corbis

Answer: The messages Muhammad received from God were recorded in the Koran.

This beautifully illuminated (decorated) copy
of the Koran was made in the 18th century
for the sultan of Morocco.
© Corbis

SEARCH LIGHT

True or
false?
Muhammad
wrote down
the entire Koran.

Holy Book of Islam

Followers of the religion called Islam (Muslims) believe that God spoke to the Prophet Muhammad through the angel Gabriel. Muhammad received these messages for about 20 years. God, called Allah in Arabic, sent the

messages so that Arabs would have a holy book in their own language. Muhammad and his followers memorized the messages and sometimes wrote them down. Altogether they're called the Koran, or Qur'an, which means '**recitation**' or 'reading' in Arabic.

After Muhammad's death, Muslims were afraid that the knowledge in the Koran would be lost. So Uthman, the third caliph (Islamic ruler), ordered a single, official version of the Koran to be created.

The Koran's 114 chapters are not presented in the order they were revealed to Muhammad. The chapters are called *surah*s. The *surah*s have different lengths, but each begins with a prayer and is written in a poetic tone.

According to the Koran, there is only one God and all Muslims should obey God and his word. The Koran also reflects a belief in the

(Top) Young Nigerian girl reads the Koran with other students. (Bottom) Students in Islamabad, Pakistan, at a *madrasah* (Muslim school of higher learning).

resurrection from the dead, in angels and devils, and in heaven and hell. All people will be judged by God. The book also says that God's message to Muhammad is both a warning and a promise. It's a warning to those who refuse to believe in the one God. But it also promises spiritual rewards to those who believe in God and do his will.

For Muslims, the Koran is the true word of God and the final word in all matters of law and religion. It is also considered to be without any error in what it teaches.

LEARN MORE! READ THESE ARTICLES...
BIBLE (VOLUME 5) • CAIRO, EGYPT (VOLUME 8)
MUHAMMAD (VOLUME 5)

DID YOU KNOW?
Many inside and outside portions of the Taj Mahal in India are inlaid with verses of the Koran. Calligraphy (artistic lettering) is a major Islamic art form. Some forms of Islam do not allow artistic images of living things, though the Koran does not mention this.

Answer: FALSE. Muhammad wrote down some of the holy messages he received. But one of Muhammad's successors, Uthman, ordered that the contents of the Koran be collected and written down.

A Simple Faith

The Baha'i faith is a fairly new religion with followers throughout the world. It grew out of Islam, the religion founded by Muhammad. After Muhammad's death, the Islamic religion split into two groups, Sunnites and Shiites. Some Muslims (as followers of Islam are called) used the title of 'bab' (Arabic for 'gateway') for their religious leaders. The most famous use of the term was by a Persian (Iranian) Shiite named Mirza Ali Mohammad, who declared himself 'the Bab' in 1844.

Abd ol-Baha (Abdul Baha), first leader of the Baha'i faith, who is called the 'Centre of the Covenant' and 'Architect of the Administrative Order'.
© Baha'i World Centre

One of the Bab's earliest followers was Mirza Hoseyn Ali Nuri, who took the name Baha Ullah. In 1863 he declared himself to be the messenger of God whom the Bab had predicted would come. Most of the Bab's followers believed him. Baha Ullah later founded the Baha'i faith. He made his eldest son, Abd ol-Baha (Abdul Baha), the leader of the Baha'i community.

The Baha'i faith teaches that a person's purpose in life is to worship God through prayer and meditation and seeks to unite all people in one religion. Those who follow this faith believe that people must also work to end racial, class, and religious unfairness. They believe that the founders of the world's great religions are all messengers of God. These messengers include Moses, the Buddha, Jesus, Muhammad, and Baha Ullah. They also believe there will be more messengers of God in the future. Followers of this religion do not drink alcohol, and they must seek permission from parents to marry.

Baha'i followers attend local spiritual assemblies to worship. There are also several impressive Baha'i temples located around the world. Baha'i services are extremely simple. There is no preaching. Instead, there are readings from the scriptures.

DID YOU KNOW?
Most Baha'i temples are nine-sided domes. These features suggest both the differences between and the unity of all people.

LEARN MORE! READ THESE ARTICLES...
ARCHITECTURE (VOLUME 3) • IRAN (VOLUME 7)
ISLAM (VOLUME 5)

The Baha'i House of Worship in Wilmette, Illinois, U.S., is one of seven throughout the world - at least one on each continent.
© Richard Hamilton Smith/Corbis

SEARCH LIGHT

Fill in the gaps:

_____ was the founder of the Baha'i faith.

Teacher of Great Wisdom

Confucius was a Chinese teacher and thinker. He believed in understanding and learning, and in people's ability to improve themselves. In China, Confucius' ideas have been important for thousands of years. There, he is known as Kongzi, which means 'Master Kong'.

Confucianism is often called a religion, but it is really a system of **values** for living a good life. Confucius spoke more about goodness than about God. His teaching focused on how people could make themselves better in their lifetimes. He also taught about the importance of honouring one's parents and ruler.

Confucius was born to a poor family in 551 BC, more than 2,500 years ago. His father died when he was 3 years old. After that his mother educated him in music, shooting with a bow and arrow, arithmetic, chariot riding, and calligraphy (the art of handwriting). Confucius also studied Chinese poetry and history. All these things helped him become a good teacher.

In China during Confucius' time, parents sometimes hired special **tutors** to educate their

SEARCH LIGHT

Confucius was mostly concerned with
a) learning and money.
b) learning and self-improvement.
c) animals and learning.

children. Only the wealthy could afford tutors, and poor children had fewer chances for education. Confucius wanted to make education available to all because he believed everyone needed to acquire knowledge and build character. He believed that education was the best way to understand yourself and improve the world.

Confucius spent his whole life learning and teaching so that he could change society for the better. Many of his wise sayings were collected in a work called the *Analects*. Today, many East Asian countries celebrate Confucius' birthday as a holiday.

LEARN MORE! READ THESE ARTICLES…
CHINA (VOLUME 7) • DALAI LAMA (VOLUME 5)
SOCRATES (VOLUME 4)

DID YOU KNOW?
You may have heard of one of Confucius' famous sayings: 'A journey of a thousand miles begins with a single step.' What do you think he meant by that?

Answer: b) learning and self-improvement.

The Religion of Laozi

Over 2,500 years ago, there lived a wise **philosopher** in China. His name was Laozi. Laozi (also spelled Lao-tzu) lived in a time of battles and great social troubles. His teachings, therefore, offered a way to bring nature and human life into harmony.

The teachings of Laozi and others became the religion known as Daoism (or Taoism). According to Daoist tradition, Laozi wrote a book on Daoism known as *Daodejing*, or 'Classic of the Way of Power'. The main purpose of this book was to advise the king on how to rule his kingdom.

The *Yin* and *Yang* symbol, suggesting the way opposites join to make up the wholeness of life.

Today Laozi is honoured as a saint by his followers in mainland China, Taiwan, Vietnam, Japan, and Korea. The followers of Daoism believe in the Dao (meaning the 'way'), which is understood as a natural force and the source of all things in the universe. In Daoism death is a natural process and results in a person's returning to his or her source, the Dao.

Daoism states that a human being is part of a universe based on the spiritual principles of *Yin* and *Yang*. *Yin* and *Yang* mean the 'dark side' and 'sunny side' of a hill. Together they create the wholeness of nature. A human being carries both *Yin* and *Yang* in his or her body and must balance them in daily activities through personal discipline.

While Daoism teaches the freedom of the individual, it also stresses the duties of the community toward its people and the duties of government toward its citizens. This is just one more example of the balance of *Yin* and *Yang*.

Daoism and Confucianism are very different systems. But together, for thousands of years, they have been major influences on Chinese culture.

LEARN MORE! READ THESE ARTICLES...
BUDDHISM (VOLUME 5) • CHINA (VOLUME 7) • CONFUCIUS (VOLUME 5)

SEARCH LIGHT

Daoism began in
a) China.
b) Vietnam.
c) Korea.

During the Chinese New Year celebration, Daoists in Kowloon pray and make offerings at the Wong Tai Sin temple.
© Dave G. Houser/Corbis

DID YOU KNOW?
In Daoist belief, *Yin* is thought of as earth, female, and dark. It is represented by the tiger, the colour orange, and a broken line. *Yang* is thought of as heaven, male, and light. It is represented by the dragon, the colour azure, and an unbroken line.

In Shinto tradition, Inari is the god of rice cultivation and merchants. The Fushimi Inari shrine near Kyoto, Japan, is one of the most famous of many Inari shrines.
© David Samuel Robbins/Corbis

SEARCH LIGHT

True or false?
In Shintoism, forces of nature may be worshipped.

A Very Japanese Religion

Nearly all the followers of the Shinto religion are natives of a single country: Japan. There is no clear indication when Shinto began. It is basically as ancient as the Japanese people themselves.

Shinto is a loose set of beliefs and attitudes held by most Japanese about themselves, their families, and their ancestors. Shinto has no central

Shinto monk visits shrine on Mount Haguro in Japan.
© Chris Rainier/Corbis

holy book. No single group or individual created the religion. But its beliefs were strongly influenced by several Eastern religions. These include Confucianism, Daoism, and Buddhism. In fact, most Shinto followers are also active Buddhists.

Shintoists honour and worship powers called *kami*. These may be gods, forces of mercy, certain ancestors, or other powers considered to be **divine**. *Kami* can't be known or explained. But they are believed to be the source of human life. And they guide people to live in harmony with the truth.

Each family or community has a specific *kami* that acts as the group's guardian. Many *kami* are connected to objects and creatures of nature, as well as to particular areas and family groups. Believers' own ancestors are also deeply honoured and worshipped.

Unlike many religions, Shinto has no regularly scheduled services or meetings for worship. Worshippers may visit their *kami's* **shrines** (or others) anytime they want to - some go every day. Several festivals and ceremonies during the year bring believers together. Shintoists celebrate births and weddings in special ceremonies.

The major Shinto celebrations are the Spring Festival, the Autumn Festival (a kind of harvest festival), and the Annual Festival (New Year celebration) with a Divine Procession, or parade. Each grand festival has a specific order of **rituals** to be carried out.

LEARN MORE! READ THESE ARTICLES...
BUDDHISM (VOLUME 5) • CONFUCIUS (VOLUME 5)
JAPAN: MODERN NATION OF ANCIENT
TRADITIONS (VOLUME 7)

DID YOU KNOW?
In Shinto mythology, the sun goddess Amaterasu has long held a special place. She is the guardian *kami* of the Japanese royal house.

Answer: TRUE.

DID YOU KNOW?
Hindus consider the Ganges River, or Ganga, to be a holy place. Every year, hundreds of thousands of people bathe in the Ganges during a festival called a *mela*.

Ancient Religion of South Asia

Hinduism is a religion, but it is also a culture and a way of life. Over 800 million people, mostly in India and Nepal, practise Hinduism.

The roots of Hinduism go back more than 3,000 years. Since that time it has grown into many different **sects**. The beliefs of one Hindu might not be the same as those of another. But Hinduism is generally very accepting of differences between these subgroups.

Hindu devotees pray as they bathe in the holy Ganges River.
© AFP/Corbis

Brahman is the one supreme power in Hinduism, but most Hindus believe there are many gods. Most important among these gods are Vishnu, Shiva, Brahma, and Shakti. Each of the different gods has influence over a different part of life. For example, the elephant-headed god Ganesha helps remove difficulties. Lakshmi is the goddess of wealth. Shiva is one of the main and most complex Hindu gods. He both destroys things and rebuilds them.

Meditation is a very important part of Hinduism. It encourages relaxation and concentration to free the mind. Other forms of worship include chanting hymns and performing small **sacrifices** to the gods. There are also many holy books in Hinduism. The most famous and important one is the Bhagavadgita.

Most Hindus believe that human souls are reborn after death. The Hindu law of *karma* says that what a person does in one life affects his or her future life. In Hinduism the purpose of life is to do good things in order to free yourself from the cycle of rebirth.

Another important Hindu view is *ahimsa*, which means 'non-injury' to all living things. This has led to the well-known Hindu respect for the cow.

LEARN MORE! READ THESE ARTICLES...
MAHATMA GANDHI (VOLUME 4) • INDIA (VOLUME 7) • JAINISM (VOLUME 5)

SEARCH LIGHT

Fill in the gap. The Hindu concept of *karma* has to do with the cycle of _____.

The major Hindu goddess Kali is shown here in the Sri Veeramakaliamman Temple in Singapore. Like many Hindu gods and goddesses, Kali is described as having opposing qualities. For instance, Kali is linked with both violence and motherly love.
© Ted Streshinsky/Corbis

SEARCH LIGHT

Where did the Buddha live and teach?

DID YOU KNOW?

The Leshan Buddha in Sichuan, China, is the tallest statue of Buddha in the world, even though it is in a seated position. It is over 71 metres tall. More than 100 people can stand on one of the statue's feet.

In southwestern China, Buddhists may worship at temples such as this one in Kunming, in Yunnan province.
© Royalty-Free/Corbis

80

The Teachings of the Buddha

The religion that developed in ancient India around the teachings of Siddhartha Gautama, the Buddha, is called Buddhism. His teachings offered a way to achieve **Enlightenment**, and he attracted many followers. After his death, temples were built in his honour and his religion spread through much of Asia, especially China, Korea, and Japan. It has spread to Western countries too.

The Buddha taught about the Four Noble Truths, which became the basis of Buddhism. The First Noble Truth is that life is made up of pain and suffering. The Second Noble Truth is that all suffering is caused by a person's desires, by wanting. The Third Noble Truth is that a person can be free from these self-centred desires. The freedom from desire is called Nirvana, or Enlightenment. The Fourth Noble Truth is called the Eightfold Path.

To follow the Eightfold Path means that a person follows a Middle Way between a life of luxury and a life of unnecessary poverty. Following this path eventually leads to a life free from suffering. The eight parts of the Path are: right understanding (of the Four Noble Truths), right thought, right speech, right action (including non-violence), right way of living (occupations in line with Buddhist beliefs), right effort, right mindfulness (attention), and right concentration (**meditation**).

© Alison Wright/Corbis

© Richard Bickel/Corbis

(Top) Buddhist nuns in Dharmshala, India, where Tibet's Dalai Lama and others fled from their homeland in 1959. (Bottom) Student monks holding bowls to receive alms (offerings) in Bagan, Myanmar.

The Buddha's teachings weren't written down until 300 years after his death. By then the religion had split into a number of groups, each with a different understanding of the Buddha's teachings. And today Buddhist monks, nuns, and priests carry the teachings forward as they understand them.

LEARN MORE! READ THESE ARTICLES...
BASHO (VOLUME 3) • KATHMANDU (VOLUME 7) • SHINTO (VOLUME 5)

Answer: The Buddha lived and taught in ancient India.

The Enlightened One

DID YOU KNOW?
The teachings of the world's great religious leaders often overlap. The Buddha taught that people should 'consider others as yourself'. Similarly, Jesus Christ taught that people should 'do unto others as you would have others do unto you'.

The term 'buddha' means '**enlightened** one' - one who understands truths beyond the everyday world. It is not a name but rather a title of respect. 'The Buddha' or the name Gautama refers to the founder of the religion called Buddhism. If you see an image of him, he looks peaceful, wise, and full of love.

Gautama was the son of a king. He was born long ago near what's now the border of Nepal and India. His personal name was Siddhartha. Before his birth, his mother had a strange dream about a beautiful white elephant. The holy men predicted that the queen would have a son who would grow up to be either a king or a buddha.

When he was 29 years old, Siddhartha saw four sights that left him thinking about the purpose of life. He saw a weak old man with a walking stick. Another day he saw a sick man, and another day a dead body. Then Siddhartha saw a holy man looking very calm.

Siddhartha decided to give up the life of a prince. He left his home in search of truth. At one point he decided to sit under a tree until he became enlightened. He wanted to understand the truth about the spirit and about life. Finally, at the age of 35, Siddhartha reached enlightenment. He became the Buddha. The tree he sat under is called the bodhi ('enlightenment') tree.

Buddha spent the rest of his life teaching people a way of thought and living that involved **meditation** and a freedom from suffering. While he did not claim to be a god, some people do pray to him. Many people live their lives according to Buddhist teachings.

SEARCH LIGHT

Fill in the gaps. The word 'buddha' means '_____ _____'.

LEARN MORE! READ THESE ARTICLES...
ASHOKA (VOLUME 4) • BUDDHISM (VOLUME 5) • INDIA (VOLUME 7)

Answer: The word 'buddha' means 'enlightened one'.

Which of
the following
is a good
translation of the
title Dalai Lama?
a) religious leader
b) yellow teacher
c) wisest teacher

DID YOU KNOW?
In 1989 the present Dalai Lama was
awarded the Nobel Prize for Peace.
This honoured his non-violent efforts
to end Chinese domination of Tibet.

Tibet's Great Teacher

The word *lama* means 'teacher' in the Tibetan language. Lamas are religious leaders who are usually great teachers or heads of **monasteries**. In the Mongolian language, *dalai* means 'ocean', and stands for a vast 'sea of wisdom'. The Dalai Lama is head of the leading Tibetan Buddhist group called the Yellow Hat order. He's also the religious leader of Tibet. Until 1959, the Dalai Lama was the head of the Tibetan government as well.

Children observing the 14th Dalai Lama as he visits Sarnath, Uttar Pradesh, India, in January 2003.
© AP/Wide World

Tibetans believe that some lamas are reborn as other lamas. The Dalai Lama is considered to be the human form of Avalokiteshvara. Avalokiteshvara is a *bodhisattva* (a Buddha-to-be) known especially for his kindness and mercy towards humans. The first Dalai Lama was Dge-'dun-grub-pa. All the Dalai Lamas that followed him are believed to be his reincarnations (rebirths).

How do the Tibetans know that the Dalai Lama has been reborn? The rebirth may happen days or even years after a Dalai Lama has died. Special attention is paid to a dying Dalai Lama's words and to any unusual signs during his death. Also, one special priest is believed to have visions and other **mystical** knowledge about a newly reborn Dalai Lama. A careful search based on these clues takes place. Often two or more boys may be examined before the new Dalai Lama is finally announced. The new Dalai Lama is trained at a monastery from an early age. A chosen adult rules the state until the young Dalai Lama has been educated.

Since 1959, the present (14th) Dalai Lama has lived in **exile** in Dharmsala, India. He and some followers left after a failed Tibetan rebellion against the Chinese government, which had invaded Tibet in 1950. Since then the Dalai Lama has worked hard but peacefully for Tibet's independence.

LEARN MORE! READ THESE ARTICLES...
BUDDHISM (VOLUME 5) • CHINA (VOLUME 7) • MONASTICISM (VOLUME 5)

The present Dalai Lama teaches, lectures, and speaks to thousands of people worldwide. If he had not been exiled from Tibet, he would have led a quiet and protected life. But today he is a popular and well-spoken representative of the Buddhist religion and Tibetan independence.
© AP/Wide World

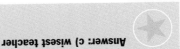

Answer: c) wisest teacher

DID YOU KNOW?
Jain non-violence includes insects. Many monks own nothing but a small broom to sweep insects from their paths and a mouth-and-nose covering to prevent them from swallowing or inhaling small insects.

Teaching Non-violence

SEARCH LIGHT

Jainism is one of three major ancient religions of India, along with Buddhism and Hinduism. Jainism was founded more than 2,500 years ago by Mahavira. He probably lived at the same time as Siddhartha Gautama, who founded Buddhism.

The term Jainism comes from the word Jina, which means 'conqueror'. Jains believe that it is possible to fight earthly desires and physical needs to reach a stage of perfect understanding and purity. They work towards this **perfection** by taking vows that help them live properly. Jains try to reach a point where they no longer depend on the world or their bodies for anything. A person who reaches this stage is called a Jina.

True or false? Jains are vegetarians.

In Jainism all living things have value. Jains believe in *ahimsa*, or non-violence, which means they cannot harm any living creature. As a result of this belief, most Jains are **vegetarians**.

Jainism has both **lay** followers (regular believers) and monks and nuns. All Jains are forbidden to lie, steal, and eat meals at night. But Jain monks and nuns also follow other very strict rules as they try to achieve a perfect inner state. They do not marry, and they keep few or no possessions. Most Jains are lay followers. They may marry, but they are expected to avoid certain foods and to keep few possessions. They are also expected to avoid unnecessary travel and pleasure, to **fast**, and to serve their fellow Jains, especially the monks and nuns and the poor.

Jain worshipper pouring a milk offering on a huge Indian statue of Bahubali, the first human of this world-age to gain perfection and release from worldly needs.
© Chris Lisle/Corbis

Many lay followers also worship or make offerings to past Jinas and to various gods and goddesses. There are about 4 million followers of Jainism today in India and 100,000 in other countries.

LEARN MORE! READ THESE ARTICLES...
ASIA (VOLUME 7) • BUDDHISM (VOLUME 5) • INDIA (VOLUME 7)

This Jain priest stands before a statuette of Mahavira, founder of Jainism. His name means 'great hero', and he is honoured as the last of the 24 Jinas.
© Charles & Josette Lenars/Corbis

Answer: TRUE. Most Jains do not eat meat.

A South Asian Religion

SEARCH LIGHT

Which of the following is the holy book of the Sikhs?
a) Guru Nanek
b) *Adi Granth*
c) Amritsar

Sikhism is a religion founded by Guru Nanak in the late 15th century in India. The word 'guru' means 'teacher'. The word 'Sikh' means 'disciple' or 'learner'.

Guru Nanak was the first Sikh guru. There were nine gurus after him. The fifth Sikh guru, Arjun, wrote down his own **hymns** and those of the earlier gurus. The last guru, Gobind Singh (also called Gobind Rai), added his own hymns. He said that after his death the book in which the hymns were written would take the place of the Sikh guru. This book became the holy book of the Sikhs, called the *Adi Granth*, or *Granth Sahib*.

Sikhs call their places of worship *gurdwara*s ('gateways to the guru'). The chief *gurdwara* is the Golden Temple, built in 1604 in Amritsar, India.

Teacher helping two Sikh boys with lessons.
© Annie Griffiths Belt/Corbis

Sikhs eat together in the *gurdwara* as a sign of the equality of all kinds of people.

Sikhism includes **aspects** of two other religions, Hinduism and Islam. From Hinduism comes belief in a cycle of birth, death, and rebirth. Another Hindu feature is the concept of *karma*, which says that a person's previous life affects the present one. Islam's influence can be seen in Sikhism's description of God as the One, the Truth, the Creator, the immortal, the formless, and the ever present.

Most Sikh boys and girls will become part of the Khalsa, the Sikh **order** of soldier-scholar-saints. After that, men must not cut their hair, must wear short trousers (even under their longer outer trousers) and a steel bracelet, and must carry a comb and a sword. Sikhs are not permitted to use liquor, tobacco, or drugs.

LEARN MORE! READ THESE ARTICLES…
HINDUISM (VOLUME 5) • INDIA (VOLUME 7) • ISLAM (VOLUME 7)

Much of Sikh worship is an individual activity. This woman - part of a Sikh settlement in New Mexico, U.S. - is meditating in her home.
© Buddy Mays/Corbis

DID YOU KNOW?
Dance and drama play an important part in the activities of a shaman. The north Asian shaman becomes a fascinating sight, with his cloak floating in the light of a fire. He becomes actor, dancer, singer, and storyteller.

The Spirit World

A shaman is a person believed to have extraordinary powers. 'Shaman' means 'he who knows'. It is thought that a shaman can predict what's going to happen in the future. A shaman goes into a trance to enter the spirit world and performs special rituals to cure sick people. Because of this, the shaman acts as the people's doctor and priest.

Religious beliefs in which the shaman plays a major role are called 'shamanism'. However, the believers don't refer to their belief in this way.

Shamans from Goshal village in northern India being greeted by Manali village elder (left) during festival.
© Lindsay Hebberd/Corbis

Shamanism is simply a term that groups together certain religious beliefs.

In general, followers of shamanism believe that everyone has a soul. A person falls ill when the soul leaves the body for some reason. It then becomes the job of the shaman to enter the world of spirits, get hold of the runaway soul, and bring it back to the body of the sick person.

It is believed that the spirits choose the man or woman who is to act as a shaman. The spirits first tell the person in a dream that he or she has been chosen. If the person refuses to become a shaman, he or she is made sick by the spirit until he or she gives in. People chosen as shamans typically have some unusual feature. For example, they might have an extra tooth or an extra finger.

People in very different parts of the world practise shamanism or have religions with very similar features. These include groups in North and South America, India, Australia, the Pacific Islands, and China. The greatest number of people who practise a pure shamanism live in northern Asia, mostly in the Russian region of Siberia.

LEARN MORE! READ THESE ARTICLES...
AMERICAN INDIANS (VOLUME 4) • RUSSIA (VOLUME 6) • VODUN (VOLUME 5)

SEARCH LIGHT

True or false? Shamans often have an unusual physical feature.

On the Southeast Asian island of Borneo, some people practise shamanistic traditional religions. Here a ceremonial dance is performed by a shaman of the Dayak people.
© Charles & Josette Lenars/Corbis

Answer: TRUE.

Religion of Magic and Spirits

SEARCH LIGHT

Many people in Haiti believe in the religion known as Vodun or, among most outsiders, Voodoo. Vodun came to Haiti more than 300 years ago when large numbers of people from Africa were taken there to work as slaves. As time passed, the beliefs of the African slaves mingled with those of Haiti's French plantation owners, who were mostly Roman Catholics.

Those who practice Vodun believe that there is one god and many kinds of spirits, called *loa*. The purpose of Vodun is to serve these spirits and keep their goodwill. The spirits serve as a link between people and the god whom the Haitians call Bondye.

During ceremonies the *loa* may take control of (possess) a believer. That person then may do **ritual** dances, accept animal **sacrifices** for the spirit, and offer important advice to others. Otherwise the *loa* is a combination guardian angel and **patron saint**.

A Vodun priest is called a *houngan*, and a priestess (female priest) is called a *mambo*. They lead ceremonies in which people play drums, sing, dance, pray, prepare food, and sacrifice animals. The leaders also act as counsellors, healers, and expert protectors against sorcery or witchcraft. Important Vodun spirits are honoured on feast days of different Roman Catholic saints, and the spirits of ancestors are honoured on All Saint's Day and All Souls' Day.

Many Haitians believe in zombis. A zombi is either a dead person's bodiless soul that is used for magical purposes or a dead body raised magically from the grave to be a slave.

Vodun is a mixture of African beliefs and what other religion?
a) Judaism
b) Hinduism
c) Roman Catholicism

DID YOU KNOW?
Hollywood horror movies did much to create misunderstandings about 'Voodoo' and fear of its followers. It has often been shown as an evil and terrifying religion.

LEARN MORE! READ THESE ARTICLES...
ROMAN CATHOLICISM (VOLUME 5)
SHAMANISM (VOLUME 5) • WEST INDIES (VOLUME 9)

These women in Togo, in West Africa, are being received into the Vodun tradition in a secret ritual ceremony. Many people were taken as slaves from Togo to the West Indies, where Vodun is also a major religious tradition.
© Caroline Penn/Corbis

alas unfortunately or sadly

aspect part, feature, or quality of something

commandment law or rule for living

conservative tending to safeguard existing views, conditions, or traditions

convert to win over to a new or different belief

crusade campaign or cause taken up with passion and belief

dismay sadness or disappointment

dispute to argue with

divine holy, godlike, or concerning God

Enlightenment remarkably clear state of awareness, understanding, and inner peace

exile (noun) banishment or official separation

famine drastic food shortage, often ending in starvation for many

fast (noun) period of time when a person gives up or limits eating, often for religious reasons

flask container for liquid

fleece wool of an animal such as a sheep or a goat

Gospel one of the first four New Testament books, telling of the life, death, and resurrection (raising from the dead) of Jesus Christ

hare rabbit-like animal

hermit person who has withdrawn from society to live alone

hymn song of joy or praise, often to a god

lash to tie or attach

layperson (adjective: lay) person who belongs to a religious group but is not part of its official clergy (as a priest or minister is)

magistrate official who looks after the laws of a particular area

meditation a quiet focused concentration, meant to calm and clear the mind; sometimes used to reach spiritual awareness

monastery a house for people who have taken religious vows, especially for monks

mystical having to do with a person's direct spiritual connection with a god or other supernatural power

myth story that unfolds part of the world view of a people or is used to explain a belief or natural event

order religious community, usually requiring that its members take solemn vows promising duty and faithfulness

orthodox strictly obeying traditional rules, customs, or beliefs

overseer person in charge of others who are carrying out a task

parka hooded heavy jacket for very cold weather

patron saint holy person who is chosen to specially protect a group or place

perfection state of being without flaw or error

philosopher thinker or seeker after truth and understanding of basic concepts

pilgrimage journey made to a holy place to worship there

preach to deliver a sermon; to urge to accept an idea or course of action

Promised Land in Judaism, the land of Canaan, which God promised to Abraham and Moses if the Hebrew people promised to worship only him

prophet a holy person who acts as a messenger between God and people; also, a gifted person with the ability to accurately predict future events

prosperous wealthy

psalm a sacred song or poem used in worship; especially, one of the biblical poems collected in the Book of Psalms

recitation act of speaking or reading a piece of literature aloud

resurrection raising from the dead

ritual the required form for a ceremony

sacrifice an act of offering something of value to save or make up for something else

salvation rescue from the power and effects of sin

scour to scrub hard

shrine place where honour or worship is offered to a saint or deity

staff wooden walking stick

supreme highest, best, and without limit

text written work

tolerate to put up with

tradition custom; habit of belief or of living

tutor a privately hired teacher

twilight the light between the end of day and the beginning of night; also, the name for that time of day

values morals or ideals

vegetarian a person who does not eat meat

worship (verb) to honour and show surrender and obedience to a god or supernatural power